On the Beauty of Christ and Christian Reason

Jeremy Nichols

ISBN: 0615562191
ISBN-13: 978-0615562193

Approbation

"A sincere and devout reading of the Christian revelation, and I think that the 'beautiful idea' approach might very well be as far as one can get, by explaining the power of Christianity to those who have not felt it."

Dr. Roger Scruton
- Former lecturer and professor of aesthetics at Birkbeck College, London; former professor of philosophy and university professor, Boston University; and author of over 30 books, including *Art and Imagination* (1974), *The Aesthetics of Music* (1997), and *A Political Philosophy: Arguments for Conservatism* (2006).

For those who have never believed;
For those who no longer believe;
For those who struggle to believe without a concise,
reasoned defense of their Christian faith.

On the Beauty of Christ and Christian Reason

Christians are told that those who have not seen and believe in Christ are blessed (*John 20:29*). We are also told that faith is the belief in things unseen (*Hebrews 11:1*). Because of sayings like these, it is easy to understand why we are frequently dismissed as men and women who have all "blindly" jumped into our religion.

Although our dismissal is easy to understand, it is undeserved – All Christians have not "blindly" jumped into Christianity.

Yes, there are some of us who have an unexamined, child-like devotion to Jesus (a "blind" devotion that should never be discouraged), but there are also many of us who are devoted to Christ

3

because we have followed our God-given reason –
There are many Christians who have come to Christ
with open eyes.

Today, it is particularly important to
demonstrate how Christians have used reason to
arrive at faith in Jesus Christ. After all, when modern
men and women turn to non-Christian belief systems,
they usually turn because they believe that these
systems are more reasonable than Christianity.
Arguably, in order for the good news of Christianity
to continue to comfort men and women (apart from
the occurrence of Divine revelation), Christians must
show that our faith is, in fact, very reasonable – The
only way to do this is to submit our religion to
rigorous analysis, and then to clearly communicate
the findings.

Christians do not have to be worried -
Rigorous analysis does not disprove Christianity.
Rigorous analysis (or philosophy) actually supports
Christianity. Clement of Alexandria (a Christian
writing in the 2nd century A.D.) said as much when he

wrote, "Philosophy has been given to the Greeks as their own kind of Covenant, their foundation for the philosophy of Christ." According to Clement of Alexandria, philosophy was the Greeks' special agreement with God that paved the way for Christianity. The great North African Christian, St. Augustine of Hippo, actually wrote that he credited the Greek philosopher, Plato, with his own personal quest for "invisible things understood by the things that are made" - St. Augustine thanked the philosopher, Plato, for opening the door to Christianity.

Arguably, when it comes to understanding the reasonableness of Christianity, all Christians owe Plato a debt of gratitude. However, unlike St. Augustine who thanked Plato for his thoughts on "invisible things," Christians who appreciate a reasoned defense of our faith should thank the ancient Greek philosopher for his thoughts on beauty and beautiful ideas. "Beauty," Plato wrote, "is the sign of another and higher order, and that beholding beauty with the eye of the mind you will be able to nourish true virtue and become the friend of God." For understanding the reasonableness of Christianity, it may be argued that the most useful thing Plato ever recorded was his analysis that beauty beheld with the mind enables us to be virtuous and to become the friend of God – To phrase this differently, Christianity is reasonable when we understand that beholding beauty with the eye of the mind is sacred; Christianity is reasonable when we understand that beautiful ideas are sacred.

But what is a beautiful idea? And how exactly does it enable us to nourish true virtue and to befriend God?

Like any reasonable definition of beauty, the reasonable definition of a beautiful idea must simply state that it is known when experienced; a beautiful idea is beauty experienced when thought. Because it is beauty beheld with the eye of the mind, a beautiful idea is beauty closely inspected; beauty called to answer for itself; beauty peeled by our mind's examination until nothing remains of it except that which gives us only a deep, inward feeling – Gesa Elsbeth Thiessen explained this well when she wrote, "In both Plato and Plotinus [another Greek philosopher] the vision of the beautiful is an intellectual act... as the vision of exterior beauty is only a first step before one perceives the ideas."

A beautiful idea provokes a "gut-feeling." It is the feeling that tells us that brave self-sacrifice is better than cowardly self-preservation. A man or woman only needs to compare the ugliness of an imagined rape with the beautiful idea that is an imagined newborn to know that a beautiful idea exists whether or not it can be precisely defined – To quote Gesa Elsbeth Thiessen again, the beautiful idea is "the ultimate, uniquely beautiful...that which we desire to contemplate and with which we want to be connected."

Though the beauty of brave self-sacrifice makes short work of the argument that a beautiful idea is just comfortable or sensual, it is still important to explain why a beautiful idea cannot be just an erotic idea. Yes, all beauty (including the erotic) is beauty seen with the eye of the mind. However, because beauty that is just erotic only stimulates sexual desire, it actually frustrates the mind's close inspection of it – Only when the mind can closely examine a thing of beauty can the mind uncover the beautiful idea that will provoke a deep, inward feeling. Only in those moments when the mind beholds the erotic with some distance (such as loving distance) can the mind analyze the erotic and transform it into something closer to being like the romantic; which is the beautiful idea of the erotic. Really, a beautiful idea cannot be just an erotic idea because the more an erotic idea becomes a beautiful idea the more it ceases to be just erotic (that is, the more it ceases to exist solely to stimulate sexual desire).

Significantly, our experience of the "gut-feeling" caused by a beautiful idea does not end with the sensation. According to Plato, part of what makes "beholding beauty with the eye of the mind" so important is that it nourishes virtue – We know that this is true because questioning the value of a particular beautiful idea (over-analyzing the importance of the deep, inward feeling it gives us) robs us of the very virtue associated with that particular beautiful idea.

Consider the beautiful idea of a newborn - If the examining mind does not value the "gut-feeling" it gives us, but, instead, values the question "Why do I feel so strongly about the idea of a newborn?" then the examining mind not only loses the experience of the beautiful idea of a newborn, but it also loses the ability to know the virtue in valuing a newborn for its own sake.

When a man or woman attempts to answer the question "Why do I feel so strongly about the idea of a newborn?" without regard for the beautiful idea, he or she inevitably responds with an answer that can only prompt more questions that will, in turn, prompt

9

more dissatisfying answers. For example, the man or woman might answer, "I feel strongly about the idea of a newborn because the newborn is how we continue our species." It is always the case that an answer about value that is not built upon a beautiful idea will have to answer for itself *ad infinitum, ad nauseam* (that is, long after we are sick of the questionable answers) – After all, the answer "I feel strongly about the idea of a newborn because the newborn is how we continue our species" does not tell us why it is important to continue our species.

Without appreciation for the beautiful idea, men and women cannot know what is important – Without the beautiful idea, men and women cannot know what is morally excellent and deserving of our devotion.

When Plato wrote that beholding beauty with the eye of the mind helps us to nourish true virtue, he was really saying two things: firstly, he was saying, "Follow the beautiful idea toward an encounter with virtue"; and, secondly, he was saying, "Ignore the beautiful idea at your own peril!" Plato understood that, though our mind's natural analysis of beauty is important in knowing beautiful ideas and virtues, respect for the "gut-feelings" given to us by beautiful ideas is equally important because "gut-feelings" save us (like cautionary sign-posts along a cliff's edge) from going too far with our questioning; Plato understood that our virtues exist in the beautiful ideas revealed by our curious minds and experienced by our hearts – For the sake of the deep, inward feelings given to us by the beautiful ideas; for the sake of moral excellence, Plato knew that the beautiful idea must be the last answer.

Now, before any of us (Christian or not) can apply Plato's analysis of beautiful ideas toward an understanding of Christianity, we must make two assumptions: 1) We must assume that it is better to experience a beautiful idea than to over-analyze it until there is nothing beautiful to experience; and 2) We must assume that it is better to live in a world with virtue, rather than to live in a world with only questionable answers – We must assume that the deep, inward feeling given to us by a beautiful idea is better than "going through the motions" (asking questions knowing the answers cannot ever be good enough).

Plato's analysis that beautiful ideas are sacred (that they lead us to virtue and to friendship with God) is useful for understanding the reasonableness of Christianity because rigorous analysis of Christianity reveals the most beautiful idea of God: that idea of God which is most deserving of reverence - Of course, being the most beautiful idea of God does not definitively prove that Christ is God (just like the beauty of self-sacrifice does not definitively prove its essential merit), but it does mean this: to question the divinity of Jesus Christ leaves the Christian in a world with a Creator (as there is most certainly a Creator) who does not deserve his or her devotion – The Christians' beautiful idea of God is the height of imaginable divine beauty, so much so that were Jesus Christ not God, Christians would still choose eternity with Him, rather than eternity with a Creator whose beauty had been eclipsed: a Creator whose love is questionable.

Of course, common sentiment seems to indicate that nothing eclipses the beauty of God, and this is the heart of Christian reason.

† † †

The following is my reasoned testimony of Christian faith: Christian faith attained by rigorous analysis. I hope that it (in conjunction with what I have already written here) will help Non-Christians to know Christ (or, at least, lessen the severity of their execrations); as well, I hope that it will help struggling Christians defend their faith against their own doubts in a world that is increasingly hostile to our religion.

A Reasoned Testimony

I observe the world. I see its complexity and variety, and (even though the world is brutal and seemingly unjust) it convinces me that a Creator exists.

Some religions say that the Creator is the universe. They say that God is the earth and sky; the rivers and oceans; the plants and animals; and even the people. But I cannot believe these religions – I see the way their followers diligently work to have a relationship with God, and I cannot believe that they sincerely want a relationship with a god who is also part natural disaster; part epidemic; part famine; and part genocide.

No, because all of humanity seems to want to connect with the Divine (to become, in some way, children of the God Who is love), I cannot believe that God is this cruel and, indeed, *inhuman* universe –

15

Rather, I believe that this universe is simply His creation, like a work of art.

Of course, that begs the question, "Why would a loving God make a cruel world?"

It seems to me the only answer is that He would not – Reason tells me that God made the world perfect, but something else (call it what you will; the devil, if you like) must have corrupted it.

Of course, the devil is a problem. For many, a god who permits the corruption (i.e., the suffering) the devil causes is as equally unloving as a god who, by himself, directly built corruption into his creation – For many, the question now becomes "Why would a loving God permit the devil to exist?"

There are several possible answers for why God would permit the devil to exist: 1) God, despite the logical conclusion drawn from observing the world's religious, is not all-loving; 2) God is all-loving, but He is not all-powerful; He is not powerful enough to stop the devil; or 3) God is all-loving and all-powerful, and

He permits the devil to exist for a reason justified by His love; which is the Christian answer.

Earlier, I remarked that, for many, a god who permits the corruption the devil causes is as equally unloving as a god who, by himself, directly built corruption into his creation – A closer look, however, reveals that these two ideas of the divine are not at all equal.

The idea of a god who built corruption into his creation precludes the possibility of Him being all-loving, while the idea of a god that permits the existence of the devil still admits the possibility of an all-loving and all-powerful Divinity – In the Christian idea of the Divine, God can be understood to permit the corruption of His creation *out of love* for another of His creations endowed with free will (the devil) for which corrupting God's work is a freely chosen condition of its being. In the Christian idea of the Divine, the existence of the devil's corruption in the world (creation's suffering) is not evidence of God's

17

uncaring design for the universe or of His powerlessness; it is actually proof of His truly all-embracing love: a love that accommodates even the Evil One – For Christians, the devil's existence does not mean that God has been restricted by a power greater than His; rather, it means that God has been circumscribed by God (that is, God has been reined in by His own loving will: that will with which humanity largely wishes to connect).

In order to understand how Christians can justify our faith that God is all-loving and all-powerful (as opposed to being something less beautiful), it is helpful to apply Plato's analysis of beautiful ideas[1] – If there is no respect for the beautiful idea of an omnibenevolent God, then the examining mind will over-analyze the concept of God until nothing of the Divine is sacred; if the beautiful idea of an all-loving and all-powerful God is not defended, then the

---

[1] Of course, this justification excepts experiential revelation and "blind" faith in historical Divine revelation which, for Christians, is a type of experiential revelation.

examining mind will deny us experience and knowledge of Divine sublimity.

At every step along the way toward embracing Christianity, I and others like me choose the most beautiful idea revealed by our examining minds and experienced by our hearts, rather than an infinitely questionable idea (undeserving of devotion) exposed by analysis without regard for sentiment – For many Christians like me, the path to Christ is marked by signs of beautiful ideas.

It was the English poet, John Keats (who, incidentally, was not a Christian), who wrote, "With a great poet the sense of beauty overcomes every other consideration." When we are dealing with something that we cannot definitively prove (such as the divinity of Christ), but without which we lose beauty; reasoning Christians denied experiential revelation, like the great poets, choose beauty - We choose to affirm the beauty and truth of Jesus Christ.

Before I can say more about God and the singular, distinguishing beauty of His Son, I must say something about my soul. By my conscience; by my observations; and by my reason, I am convinced that I have a soul.

Firstly, my conscience recognizes the fundamental law by which all men and women are bound ("Do unto others as you would have them do unto you.") – Significantly, recognizing this law establishes that there is a Law-Giver.

Secondly, my observations demonstrate to me that arguably everything I do (and do not do); am (and am not); think (and do not think) somehow breaks this fundamental law – I am always self-interested. Some Christians call a man or woman's unavoidable self-interest "Total Depravity"[2] – We are

---

[2] Although Roman Catholicism and Orthodoxy (among others) do not subscribe to the doctrine of Total Depravity, they still assert that the flesh and spirit are in imperfect opposition; they just do not believe this is a corruption of human nature. Fortunately, a man or woman does not have to subscribe to the doctrine of Total Depravity in order to appreciate this line of reasoning; as St. Paul wrote,

unable to obey the fundamental law because we treat everything in the world as means to ends and not simply as ends in their own right. We cannot be truly charitable because even charity must give us something in return - It must feel good.[3]

Though it is my conscience that suffers because of my moral shortcomings, my reason says that my conscience suffers for that part of me under threat

---

(*cont. from page 20*) "So I find this rule: that for me, where I want to do nothing but good, evil is close at my side. In my inmost self I dearly love God's law, but I see that acting on my body there is a different law which battles against the law in my mind. So I am brought to be a prisoner of that law of sin which lives inside my body. What a wretched man I am! Who will rescue me from this body doomed to death?" (*Romans 7:21-24*)

[3] When we recognize our "Total Depravity" (when we confess it), all men and women, regardless of religion, must also recognize that we are constitutionally incapable of damning another – As Christ said, "Let the one among you who is guiltless be the first to throw a stone" (*John 8:7*); Christ did not say this to discourage men and women from striving for moral perfection, but rather to inform our compassion toward others with heightened awareness of our own moral shortcomings.

from God's judgment for having broken His law – My reason says that my conscience suffers for my soul.

I have inherited a condition from my parents (who inherited it from their parents), a condition shared by all men and women - Some call this congenital condition "Original sin," but whatever it is called it simply means that my best intentions are not enough to spare my conscience (fearful for my soul) from the threat of Divine judgment.

Because I cannot achieve blamelessness through my own self-interested works; through my own self-interested states-of-being; through my own self-interested thoughts, I am dependent upon Another to ease my guilty mind and to defend my soul before the Law-Giver – Because only the clean can make clean the dirty, I am dependent upon God.

Acknowledging God, His law, the sorry state of my soul with respect to His law, and my need for His defense, I am able to experience the incomparably beautiful idea of Jesus Christ – The story of the boundless God (Who so loved humanity; Who so loved me) binding Himself as a human being (God's most tormented creation), and then offering Himself like a sacrificial lamb for the atonement of all our sins.

When I understand the full meaning of Christ's death on the cross, it reveals itself as the most beautiful idea a God-reverent (or God-seeking) person can know – It reveals itself as the highest Truth.

Of course, there are those who disagree.

Some disagree because they cannot understand how Christ, Who was wholly a man, could have been without sin; for them, this is too illogical.

Christians answer that Christ was without sin because he was wholly God, too. Sin is a violation of a moral rule – Men and women sin when we do not do the will of God; which is manifest on earth in ways that are different from the ideal because the world is perverted by the devil. Christ was without sin because He perfectly did the will of God in this corrupted world.

Others dispute the beauty of Christ's sacrifice because His death on the cross was barbaric and, if God is God (that is, if God is all-powerful), then it would seem that the crucifixion was completely unnecessary – "The death of Christ was not beautiful," some argue, "because men and women could have been saved in a different way."

Those who insist that men and women could have been saved differently are correct – After all, God is God and nothing is beyond His powers. However, Christ did not come for the sake of God; He did not come to serve His own limitless creative Spirit – Christ came for us.

Christ came for all of us.

And in this defiled world, there is nothing more powerful than self-sacrifice – Nothing expresses love better. In *John 15:13*, Jesus Christ even says, "No one has greater love than this, to lay down one's life for one's friends."

A mother who dies during childbirth delivers a baby who (if armed with the testimony of friends and family who were there at the event) cannot but feel its absent mother's love - Certainly, the strongest evidence that our world is broken is this: the most convincing sign of love is death.

Yes, Christ's crucifixion was barbaric; the world has never again seen such tormented selflessness. And, yes, men and women could have been saved differently; God can conceive anything – But men and women (with our limited imaginations) cannot.

Jesus Christ's loving Self-sacrifice on the cross scales the heights of our capacity to feel loved, if we are fortunate enough to allow it.[4]

---

[4] It is important to note that beholding Jesus' beauty can only take us so far – Like standing on the top rung of a ladder, having done all that we could to examine and feel for the beauty of Christ, we still need God's grace to reach down to us with His love (like a friend) in order for us to know Him (that is, in order for us to truly choose beauty). Many men and women intellectually appreciate the beauty of Christ, but cannot appreciate it otherwise; as a consequence, they cannot feel the joys and consolations that

So, I say again - Acknowledging God, His law, the sorry state of my soul with respect to His law, and my need for His defense, I am able to experience the incomparably beautiful idea of Jesus Christ – The story of the boundless God (Who so loved humanity; Who so loved me) binding Himself as a human being (God's most tormented creation), and then offering Himself like a sacrificial lamb for the atonement of all our sins.

Many skeptics try to discredit Christianity – They claim that Jesus Christ was fundamentally no different than other "Christ-like" figures in history. But the stories of other "Christ-like" figures in history never say exactly what the story of Jesus Christ says – They never talk about the boundless God binding Himself in the pained flesh of a man, and then dying for His love of our souls tormented by their inability

---

(*cont. from page 25*) Christians do - In this respect, faith in Christ will always be an undeserved blessing from God even when derived largely from analysis; in this respect, the appreciation of beauty is a revelation of God.

to fulfill Divine law. Only Jesus Christ has emerged with these characteristics.

Clever skeptics might challenge that, by this argument, a god who has died twice or three times for love of humanity deserves more reverence than Christ (even though such a god has never been recorded) – Christians simply respond, "Because God exists outside of this universe and outside of time; because God is therefore present everywhere and throughout all time; because God is as present at the crucifixion of Christ as He is with us now, then God actually endures an eternally returning death having died only once."

Bearing in mind that Christ's death is eternally returning, also consider what Christians believe Christ said at His crucifixion: "My God, my God, why have you forsaken me?" (*Matthew 27:46*). For one moment in time (a moment wherein God is forever present), Jesus cried out in doubt and despair – This means that for all time God shares in humanity's doubt and despair; He never abandons us to suffer alone.

When I think about Christ and His sacrifice, the beauty of His Spirit overcomes me; His Holy Spirit overwhelms me. Because I believe that God and Christ are One in the same (and yet necessarily distinct in order for Christ's despair on the cross to have been complete), I reason that Christ, His Holy Spirit and God are One in the same, and yet distinct – The Christian tradition calls this the Trinity. Trinitarian Christianity binds Trinitarian Protestants, Roman Catholics and Orthodox Christians as brothers and sisters in Christ.

Concerning the miracles reportedly performed by Jesus (such as His virgin birth; His healings; and His resurrection), when a man or woman, either through analysis, "blind" faith, or experiential revelation, accepts Christ's divinity, then it is not difficult to say, "Because Jesus is God, then He could have done anything no matter how seemingly impossible."

Regarding the bible, it is a fact (even supported by scripture) that there were Christ-believing men and women before there was a bible. Because of this, the bible is not required to embrace Christ's victory on the cross, though it is essential for the deepest Christian education. Those who cannot read can know (as those who could not read have known) of Jesus' sacrifice through orally and pictorially transmitted stories – The focus of the Christian faith is Christ and not a book that, however divinely inspired, is not Divine.

Though ecclesial communities (Christian communities) argue among themselves about the inerrancy of the bible and its interpretation; about the applicable laws of the bible; about the very books that constitute the bible; and about the importance of extra-biblical Christian writings, it should never be concluded by a Non-Christian that acceptance of Christ is conditional upon the resolution of these issues for him or herself – Disputes between ecclesial communities should never delay a man or woman's embracing of Christ's salvific beauty.

In reference to other religions, the reasoning Christian denied experiential revelation (like all Christians) must defend the beautiful idea – Though God has notably revealed aspects of Himself in other traditions, those purported aspects of God that challenge His immeasurable love for humanity (that deny His willingness to die for us) or that deny our salvation through the death of His Son, Jesus Christ, must be false. Again, to quote John Keats, "Beauty is truth, truth beauty, - that is all/Ye know on earth, and all ye need to know."

Jeremy Nichols
October 23rd, 2011

Feel free to e-mail Jeremy with questions and comments at nichols.jeremy.9@gmail.com, or join him on Facebook: "On the Beauty of Christ and Christian Reason"

On the Beauty of Christ and Christian Reason

www.ingramcontent.com/pod-product-compliance
Lightning Source LLC
Chambersburg PA
CBHW060645030426
42337CB00018B/3454